A FRAME LESS PERFECT

A FRAME LESS PERFECT

R.A.WHITE

Shoestring Press

Printed by imprintdigital
Upton Pyne, Exeter
www.digital.imprint.co.uk

Typesetting and cover design by The Book Typesetters
us@thebooktypesetters.com
07422 598 168
www.thebooktypesetters.com

Published by Shoestring Press
19 Devonshire Avenue, Beeston, Nottingham, NG9 1BS
(0115) 925 1827
www.shoestringpress.co.uk

First published 2022
© Copyright: R.A.White

The moral right of the author has been asserted.

ISBN 978-1-915553-11-9

ACKNOWLEDGEMENTS

The author would like to acknowledge the kind and perceptive editorial support he received from publisher John Lucas at Shoestring Press and, on earlier drafts, from Kevin Bailey and Rosalynde Price, as well as to those who provided early insights and comments over the years at Arlingtons poetry group on many of the poems.

The author would also like to thank the publishers of *Haiku Quarterly*, *The Dawntreader*, *Obsessed with Pipework* and *The First Edition* in which earlier versions of some of these poems appeared.

CONTENTS

A FRAME LESS PERFECT*

Spring blossom long gone
a small-leafed lime stands
tall against the Tudor brick

part-shading the arched door
that leads to a garden
down by the riverside

slender crown overtopping
the Deanery Tower
its spiral chimneys skewering the sky

without you a frame less perfect.

*After a painting by Thomas Gainsborough of a view of St Mary's Church
(Hadleigh, Suffolk) – then without lime tree. Sadly, the tree has recently been
cut down.

ENDING IT

The chiffon dress caresses
every possibility.
But not for him. Not now.

Leaving the office at night
a settled account; a ledger balanced
three months on, words their literal selves.

Something changed that night
the light gone. Impaled,
in darkness they stood.
                    Alone.

                              The gaze half-held;
                              a reluctant touch,
                              brushed aside

              each movement
        incrementally desensitising
              the next one

and I wonder is this how each poem must end?
however good, however fine
like the end of love, in time, its fate.

Wrung out to clichéd over familiarity

Lost in the known and knowing.

THE DECISIONS THAT WE MAKE

Tracey said 'no' to Dean
with a renaissance smile to his bold Henry
the decisions that we make
the binary code of yeses and noes
the children lost
the songs unsung
the history unmade
the lives we slip into as casually as a glove.

CATCHING THE 12:53

Through gear two bends,
the give-way tunnel at the end
running past the cast iron pillars
with their flared tops and frilled arches
the buffet breakfast menu, two sausages
two bacon, two eggs scrambled or poached
the waiting room mustily mocking our rush;
we made it just in time
suitcase wedged above your seat
tapping your iPhone
we catch a backward glance
as the 12:53 pulls out
no Brueghel moment,
no boy falling from the sky
but all the same a void of sorts
and a thought that we are all travelling fast forward
the world moving on and I am feeling nothing
the ordinary and extraordinary merging.

PLANTING GIANTS

From the new world to the old
you planted for future years
branches lifting our line of sight
from pock-marked path to summer sky
five red giants you would never see
ivy-clad offspring for another age.

WHAT WE ALWAYS KNEW
BUT COULD NOT SAY

Slate grey
          drops down to turquoise blue
                    splits to olive green

Wave on wave on shingle shore
beats hissing over green kale
Yellow Horned Poppies
and arrows of Marram
until colour drowning sound
fades like a dream
as we lay silent
only words remain
what we always knew but could not say.

UNDER ORWELL BRIDGE

The tide was too strong for you,
all your life,
but you chose to swim against the tide
not for you the green and red light limits

mud shores stretching out
to touch the river bruised to darkness
beneath the concrete arches

you chose the darker waters beyond
and now the best of you is gone,
an upturned boat cast out to sea.

HOBBY OVER LAKE

Buzzards mobbed by gulls long gone
the Hobby scythes over water
sickle-shaped wings, faster than a Swift
undercarriage white with black streaks
sharp-eyed focus:
over purple loosestrife and reeds
islands of flopped Cormorants, and fat geese
to snatch emperors and frighten kings
disturb bejewelled Damsels
glinting blue and azure
taking the morning sun.

WALKING IN JUNE

The sun shone hot that day
singeing the patches of grass
on the bridleway

a tractor tread set deep
into the biscuit-coloured earth
earth that had cracked like bone china
in the June heat

the sway of soft-feathered grasses
above a web of yarrow leaves
forming a boundary of sorts
as we walk past a field of wheat
still green to the core.

EMPTY SEAT

I could say to you that difference is good
— have a look, some time, at the edge of town

Fleabane has a radiant orange heart
and Dogrose petals are softest pink
while spikey-haired Scabious is weird looking
yet sort of cool

but the words would sound hollow
when you were the one
in your faded tartan dress and cardigan
with the empty seat next to you

each child-word stabbing you to silent disbelief
and I was not cool enough or tough enough to say:
This is wrong.

CYCLOPS AT THE MINSTREL SHOW

Tickets in hand, breathing hard, we rush past posters
promising more than Seventies beige and brown
just in time to take our seats
beneath a balcony girdled in light.

A side door swings open and dancers shimmer in
with practised smile and legs pale as moonlight
joined by straw-boatered men, their blazers candy-striped
gloved hands caressing the air; now plaintively on one knee.

A spotlight picks out blackened faces
with luminous white eyes and lips,
like parodies of miners after a shift
thrust caged and squinting into sunlight.

We sit like Cyclops;
Seeing but not seeing.

SEEING OURSELVES IN THE CATHEDRAL

Words lost in sound
we see our pixeled selves on screen
blasting the air with song

masks gone, skin tones green and red
fabrics plush-stretched to coloured strips
pew and stone merging as one

the real transposing to the unreal
and back again.

REFLECTIONS

On the bridge and looking down
they cannot see
the arches stretched below in flow of river
nothing solid, just a shimmer I suppose
but fenestrating water and light
to an oval whole.

CREATION

Among the backpacks, videos and iPhones
Ray-Bans, fast food, Capri-Suns
we inch forward.

Black uniforms wait for us
at the door:
'respectful silence please'.

Skirting stone benches carved into walls
the mirrors on castors
we look up:

at a confusion of colour, shades, shadows
nudes and prophets seated on painted architecture
the flesh, the muscle, the classical poses

to scan the vaulted curves of ceiling
until that first, almost-touch to Adam
languid and slouched on rocks
in the muted light of new beginnings.

BREAKING OUT

Free from lines of distance markers,
the pasty faces masked and in control
to reach by fifty painted arrows
in greyish light
those mosaic spots and distant eyes
uncoiled speedster stretched beneath the trees
secure from where the fear is never still.

WOMAN AS MACHINE

'Woman as machine,'
You said it softly, gazing at the collage
Hung on the crowded exhibition wall

A mad creation of cogs and wheels
Nuts and bolts and metal strips
But now I see it: flotsam rising from the deep.

CHRISTMAS AT THE CALIFORNIA

jazz flowed between the glitterballs
tables wobbling as the audience swayed
part entranced and slightly out of time

alone on podium stage you sang
with keyboard, drums, and double bass
'A Taste of Honey'
in the dregs of Christmas

then I saw it – that face shaped like yours
sat alone, indifferent to your song
impervious to the phrasing twists
your glitzy costume changes
staring at her laptop screen
tapping to another tune.

MR BLUE SKY?

Black heels, black face, black top hat,
the funeral director bowed her head
and death stood among the smiling faces
before the cardboard coffin
the sunflowers, lilies, the orchids on top.

But that is what you wanted of course.

Packed out, some sitting cross legged on the floor
a mix of eco, Brighton, London edge,
your former partner said
you were the best person he had ever known
your friends said it was your year abroad that changed you
made you sort of hippy, sort of cool, uber mum.

That would have made you happy of course.

The choir sang 'Mr Blue Sky', your favourite song
and I can still imagine you singing your heart out.

You would have loved it of course.

The humanist speaker bearded and wise
behind a cross in shadowed light
said you went much too soon
but we should celebrate your life. You having been here at all.

That is what you would have wanted of course.

Later, at a pub in Dulwich
organic quiche, egg sandwiches, roast peppers
Shiraz, merlot and vodka on the never-ending tab
among the pendants of your life hanging down
you looking back from a flat screen on the wall

would you have seen a face that had not known sleep for weeks
a mother repeating like a child
'I still cannot believe that she's not here'
and that some things cannot be made happy

However much we try.

THRESHOLDS

Past the Hadleigh, the Hanbury, and Beaulieu
the bricks, the plaster moulds, the render skim
past the Palladian nudged between a yellow-brick terrace
and a dormered three-storey block.

On to the Audi A3s and the MPVs
nestling behind rubber-leafed hedges
while a ladybird sits on a spring in a play zone
its plastic carapaces, scarlet and black.

Reaching at last a tarmac road, smooth and hard
a threshold or ending of sorts with its rampart
of sedge, wild grass tufts and thistle husks;
ten paces on, a turning that abruptly stops for now.

Then a field of winter barley that fold upon fold
breaks on wooded copse rising as an island
under a moon bulging like a dragon's eye.
Where someone told me once they found a Tudor coin.

Further still I come to seven roundels, red with white slits
next to a hard-edged block with its yellow sign
warning of death, a stick man falling down

and looking back I see the light of a hundred homes.

HUM OF THOUSANDS

Fen twilight merging reed and water
we headed home
past a bonfire amber spitting and the sound of heavy rock guitar

    to be drowned by the hum of thousands
    from ink-smudge cloud shifting liquid in the sky

        that silenced us where we stood.

THE INTERLOPERS

Shuffle left, shuffle right,
where you roosted your young
and strutted cock-sure between chimney pots
to tumble down the void
one after the other

    to fall among sofa, vases, silver photo frames

        soot stain our pictured walls
        scatter the flowers
        Jackdaws:
        bring your wildness screeching to towers of books
        fight each window-pane with beak and claw
        bring your darkness to our pastel shades

    for blackness has already come to us
    a jag-edged lumpen interloper
    has broken in with shades of night
    and all soft colours are gone

    Go quickly now:

        Get me that blanket to throw over
            your staring eyes
          to calm your fears

                to cover you in nothingness.

HEADS OF GODS

There they were: the full collection
antique gods, heads on silver coins
two Bobbies, Gordon Banks, Newton, Bell, Ball…
it seemed as though their light shone brightly
on every Esso forecourt that summer.

Never were we so good again
or so it seemed
a second empire coming
to collapse and burn in Mexico sun.

NOT FOR SALE*

You would not sell
no, not to anyone
moving from painted sketch
steamer pulling the great unseen
in light not yet blushing at her disgrace
to this, your first beloved by its side
hanging together on the gallery wall
grand to the last
gliding through waters glazed and still
all fighting spirit gone
to be timber stripped and flogged
but in your ghosted vision, co-ordinates changed
always there.

* Turner's preparatory sketch and *The Fighting Temeraire* were displayed
together at *Turner's Modern World* an exhibition curated by Tate Britain
(2020–2021).

FLATLANDS

I drove through flatlands
spiralling downwards, drifting off
       – then start –
not quite knowing how we reached this spot
of close-cropped fields and clodden mud.

YOUR FAITHFUL ENVOY

'[They have no sense of honour or jealousy]. If one of them goes along the street with his wife and meets a friend, this man will take the woman's hand and lead her aside to talk, while the husband stands by waiting until she has finished her conversation. If she takes too long about it he leaves her with the other man and goes on his way.' (*Usama Ibn Munqidh* (12th Century) translation from *The Crusades: Islamic Perspectives* Carole Hillenbrand pp347–8)

O Mighty Sultan, hear your faithful envoy
Let my tongue tell what my eyes have seen

She sways between the pillars
Her fragrance lingers in the breeze
His most precious jewel speaking to another

Free as desert wind.
Outshining the blazing sun
Her voice discovering each word anew

Seen by one and all

If such a jewel were mine
I would keep it in the blackest box
in my darkest room.

Full circle a thousand years
in this dust-stained book
your words live on

But if only I could speak to you and say:
in that imaginary act perhaps destroying
what you loved the most?

Or am I somehow missing the point
about love's DNA, its essential core?

Sofa bound and cocooned in sound
still your voice insists to be heard this Friday night
through the jazz

as I hear the heels, the chatter
the carefree slam of door.

LOSING TOUCH

Raindrops on umbrellas and bowed heads

the majorettes lay down their wreaths
with teenage cool
beneath the colours long bled out
beside the hand-carved stone
before the sister of a man
she had never known.

And I hear:
the bugle's final blast
contained to melody
'they shall not be forgotten'
a pause, before a final whistle blows;

a strand detached from its web

ever more remote.

GONE

The easy sway of your back
the pop-pop of your talk
you were always something more

younger but older than me
of course, you did not like the purple paint
my chosen shirt
heard the sound of freedom's call too soon

        leaving something smoother, colder
        harder inside

            and I am forever gone

                that me given to you.

THE GOOD COMPANION

The journey is long
the road is narrow
wrong turnings you will take
and blind bends you will follow
but never doubt you have found your good companion
for that road ahead.

A good companion for each tomorrow
to walk by your side
to choose which way to go together.

Remember you are not alone
though shadows fall
when night draws in

Jigsawed together
working as one to confront each puzzle
may our minds excite each other

Your weakness is my strength. Your strength my weakness.
Even when blisters run deep and you want to stop right there
keep going on

Diversions you will face – everyone does
but do not forget you have found your good companion
for each tomorrow.

AS THE CURTAINS CLOSE

Time
It shuffles slowly
It does not run
But it goes along its way
Time for joy, time for darkness
Time to regret
The moments you can never have back
For all you held most precious
Time to shuffle from this, your stage
At your last
And who are the faces you will see
As the curtains close
Some in the front row still
Some silent at the back
Waving or calling you home.